STOP
BEING
Predictable!

14 Tactics that will make your
Presentations
insanely effective!

Bob Boylan

Stop Being Predictable!:
14 Tactics that will make your
Presentations insanely effective!

Point Publications,
Division of Boylan Enterprises, Inc.

1st Edition
Copyright © Bob Boylan 2011
424 Settlement Lane
River Valley Ranch, Carbondale, Colorado 81623

International Standard Book Number: ISBN 978-0-615-50925-9
Library of Congress Catalogue Card Number: 2011933628

Author: Bob Boylan
bobboylan@me.com   www.bobboylan.com

Interior Illustrations by © Jack Linstrum
and © Jerry Begly

Book Design by Linda J. Fleming

Author Photograph by Linda Boylan

Also by Bob Boylan:

Get Everyone in Your Boat Rowing in the Same Direction:
5 Leadership Principles to Follow So Others Will Follow You

What's Your Point?:
The Method for Making Effective Presentations

Acknowledgements

The key people that have made this book possible are my clients.

I have enjoyed 100% repeat /referral for over 30 years
in my training /consulting business.
That fact would not have happened if my training did not "take."

For "Training to Take" the ideas must be transferred and made part of
how a person presents on a regular basis.

My clients have provided me the laboratory for my ideas to be
field tested so they work. Predictably work! My clients have taken
the risks to try them and have been rewarded with better outcomes.

The examples in this book are real life presentation "war stories."
I have intentionally left off the specific clients' names
since the stories involve serious presentations
that contain confidential information.

Linda Fleming handled the design and production
of this book. So how it looks is to her credit.

Charlie Wertheim edited this book to make it as clear
and concise as possible.

Jerry Begly and Jack Lindstrom created the cartoons.
Their ability to help me make my books more
visually interesting is self-evident.

It goes without saying that my wife, the Reverend
Linda Boylan, supports and encourages me
to follow what I believe I should do.
Her kindness and love make projects like this a work of joy.

My core ability to be an inspiring coach.
I pray that the users of the ideas in this book
will let me hear their outcomes. That is my "real pay."

◆◆◆

Dedication

— I want to dedicate this book to my former pastor and mentor,
Father Arnold Weber.

— Father Arnold is a Benedictine priest who has had
an enormous influence on my life.

— He has told me more than once, "You know, Bob, to know
and not do is to not know. Why know something and not do it.
It just clutters up your brain, Bob!"

— So I have felt responsible to share what I do know
that works in my main field of concentration
in my professional life: Presenting.

— I wanted to share these ideas because I know they work.

— It was necessary for me to "Go DO" this book
so hopefully more people who really care about
their idea of the moment will have a better chance
to make their idea become reality.

— "Creativity" is thinking of new things.
"Innovation" is doing new things.
The world is not short of creativity.
But I have experienced we are very short of
making these ideas become reality.

—You will decide if you help the listeners
to your presentation better "see" the passion
you have for your idea and
how it can help them.
Then innovation will have happened and
we will all be demonstrating
Father Arnold Weber's great wisdom.

Thanks, Father Arnold!

Table of Contents

Use this resource guide in any order you wish

INTRODUCTION

You are ready to give an important presentation.

You know your stuff. You've honed your thoughts. You believe you have a good idea. You have created great visuals. You have included everything others in your organization believe you should say. You have rehearsed.

In fact, you even sense that this particular presentation is more important than others you have given lately.

Your presentation may be to one person internally. It may be to a vendor. It may be to a group of customers. It may be to a prospect. It may be to your manufacturing people. It may be to your boss.

You also know that this presentation is pretty much like all the others you give.

Professionally adequate, yes, but not a whole lot different from the presentations you have given before and probably not much different than the presentations other folks give.

You will come off professional and well-prepared. Ideally, even excited about your idea.

The problem is you will be just about what they expect.

The information will sound similar to what they have heard before. The ideas will feel fairly commodity-like, even when they are not. The delivery will be quite predictable, and the visuals will be what they expect. "Wow, another PowerPoint presentation. How exciting," they say to themselves with a yawn as you begin.

You can make your presentation insanely effective.

By doing so, you will dramatically improve the chance of getting your recommendation approved.

This book is about simple ways to make your presentation stand out from the rest by stepping away from the familiar, predictable patterns.

If you stop being predictable, you will come across as:

More memorable
More focused
More interesting
More real
More engaging
More energized
More conversational/less presentational

Realize . . .

A great presentation can break the listeners' petrified opinions.
A great presentation can set new targets.
A great presentation unlocks the power of a dream.
A great presentation can help listeners realize they can make major strides by making some changes.
A great presentation can inspire action.
A great presentation gets people moving. Off the dime moving!
A great presentation will get you noticed.

Most presenters are very competent, just as you are. However, most presenters do things in about the same way. They are anything but interesting and memorable. They win their share but they could be MUCH more successful . . . **MUCH MORE.**

Almost everyone presents in a similar fashion. If you doubt this, think about the presentations you have given lately or listened to. They are typically "data dumps" with nothing but information, usually exclusively in PowerPoint slides, heaped on the listeners until the listeners' brains ache and they find themselves well past overload.

Through the experience of helping my clients have the best possible chance to win big proposals, I have learned one strategy over and over again:

If you want to make your presentation insanely effective, you must stop being predictable.

You Must.

Period.

You must, OR your chance of winning is purely a function of the percentage of how many are presenting for this opportunity, i.e., when you are one of four presenters, you have a 25% chance of winning.

You will improve that percentage IF you stop being predictable.

I have been a presentation trainer of middle to top management for more than 30 years. I know the ideas in this book deliver when you are on the line presenting in some conference room. I just plain know they work because they have worked for my clients. And I get hired back, which is the ultimate measurement.

The problem summarized

The problem is predictability.

The problem is not enough time to be creative.

The problem is you are comfortable with how you have presented hundreds of times before.

The problem is your fear of presenting anything that is different from what you believe the listener expects.

The problem is simply not doing something different because it involves change.

The problem is you are not used to going outside the box on most things in your life.

That's normal.

However, the problem with staying put in old ways and not embracing risk is that you will not make significant change. You won't lead effectively. And your stimulating idea won't live because you presented it like all the others and no one got it!
And even if you thought of doing something differently this time, you're not sure what to do to stand out from the crowd anyway. Plus, it's time to present tomorrow!

That's where this reference guide-style book comes in handy.

Each of the 14 tactics
is arranged as follows:

Typical situation
(This may bring tears/laughter because you will recognize yourself.)

The actual tactic

A real-life story using the tactic

So what can you do right now
to use the idea?
(A step-by-step "to do list" to execute this idea within 24 hours or less)

By the way, since each tactic can be executed within 24 hours or less, you can spend your time executing and delivering more effective presentations, rather than reading about how to be more effective.

When you ponder the sameness of the 30 million PowerPoint presentations that take place daily, you will realize it is downright necessary to be different to gain the understanding, interest, involvement, shared energy, and memorability that convince listeners to act on your recommendation.

You won't have to ask anyone if there was a difference. You will instantly discover the difference based on how you feel and based on the results you see. Then you will try more of the ideas in your next presentation. Soon it will become second nature to do things differently.

In his book "Differentiate or Die," Jack Trout sums up how you will discover the necessity of differentiating in order to realize the success you desire. If you don't go "out there" and differentiate, you will feel you're not impacting anyone and may as well go away (to die).

Almost everyone agrees that today's marketplace is more competitive than it used to be. This fact creates the necessity for new ideas to be not just a little off center, but substantially different.

They must be markedly less predictable so that there is a new and clear competitive difference to your presentation.

Therefore, by definition, ideas in today's marketplace have to be risky in order to cause change that is substantive.

And yet we continue to present these dazzling, new, fresh and innovative ideas in the same way we always have.

The world is not short of creativity (new ideas). However, the world falls well short of innovatively presenting these ideas in a way that gives them a fighting chance to live and to benefit those they were intended for.

That is why I believe you are shirking your responsibility if you continue to present in the "same old way."

Stop being predictable

and increase your chance of people buying in and acting!

The 14 tactics in this book will help you stand out from your competitors, and you will reap the benefits.

The most significant benefit will be better outcomes.

The outcome is the thing to focus on. What happens after someone gives a presentation? Were they successful?

For 30 years my company's name has been "Successful Presentations." But my focus is on successful outcomes.

In "The 7 Habits of Highly Successful People," Steven Covey states that Habit 2 means to "Begin with the End in Mind." When presenters keep the end in mind while planning what they are going to say and do, they'd better be clear about just how much they really care about the idea. They have to know without a doubt that they are presenting because they see a better end in mind for the listener.

When you care in your gut and you discover you really do give a rip, you will give every ounce of your fabric to get the listener to understand your idea, and understand why it will be beneficial and what steps need to be taken next to make the idea become reality.

Plain old presenting in the predictable fashion you have done in the past will not improve the outcome.

With your focus on outcome, you will naturally gravitate away from giving predictable presentations, so you will have a better chance to attain the desired outcome.

Now select one or more of the 14 tactics to make your presentation insanely effective and experience a dramatically improved chance of success!

Tactic:1

Focus on them,
not you.

Typical Situation

Thank you very much for allowing me to present to you today. Our company has handled many issues similar to yours, and we are confident our processes and technology can move your organization forward, so you can meet the challenges you have described to us. We have helped others like you before, and we can help you, too.

Let me review what we have done and why our people and our processes are so revolutionary.

"I! WE! OUR!"

First of all, our people are special.

Special because they have more experience than their counter parts in other firms in our industry. They are constantly being trained at our own state-of-the-art corporate training center, where we employ the finest trainers and have at our people's disposal simply the best research minds in our industry.

Second, there's our commitment to service beyond the norm. We call it Unlimited Service. What a response we are having from our customer base to that concept! It has set us apart from others, pure and simple.

Now regarding our value to your firm, just let me say that we have some benchmarks of how we have delivered to the bottom line of our customers. Let me illustrate how we have used our unique service and technology to advance the ball for firms like yours. . . .

And so it goes. Lots of terrific information about your organization. That is how many presenters begin. Maybe most presenters. It is almost predictable, and many listeners even encourage it by asking you, "Will you please tell us about your organization, because not everyone has met you yet?"

Presenters accept the invitation and leap into a well-produced and usually well-delivered presentation with beautiful visuals, all designed to evangelize your organization's products and services.

It sounds like this . . .

In fact I (we) have not met all of you before, so let me first tell you about our organization, so you can understand all we bring to the table.

Sound familiar?

Tactic:1
Focus on them, not you.

Listeners ache to have us talk about their needs, but presenters tend to keep the focus on their own company and will do almost anything to talk about what they want to say. Whether you are presenting to change someone's opinion, change an attitude, change some processes, close a deal, or sell your services or products, almost all presenters start out by reviewing their background and experience and their organization's capabilities and successes.

Even custom dog-and-pony shows representing months of research and work by your team won't win customers if you focus on your own products, processes, and organization, rather than on your potential client's needs and concerns. Instead, begin with a very clear statement of your client's needs, outlined on a flip-chart page, and use this as the agenda for your presentation. You will find that the same people, wearing the same clothes, presenting to the same sorts of customers the same products, price points, experiences, and abilities will dramatically increase your win rate.

Instead, begin with your listeners' needs.

...Listeners ache to have us talk about their needs ...

A Real-Life Story

A few years ago I got a call from the West Coast office of one of the top five advertising agencies in the world.

The head of business development said that, in the past nine months, he and his team had gone zero-for-sixteen in new business presentations. These were not just capability presentations, but custom dog-and-pony shows representing months of research and work by the team, which was competing in the final round with three or four other agencies.

When I arrived, I found a group of unhappy campers. All of these people were professionals. They knew they were very good, but they weren't winning. They felt angry and frustrated. It soon became clear that, in their presentations, these people were focusing on their own products, processes, and organization, rather than on the potential client's needs and concerns. This is business as usual today: a well-produced media presentation using all the grandeur of PowerPoint to blast out the story of your own organization.

I suggested they begin their presentations in a different manner and with a different content. I suggested they begin with a very clear statement of their client's needs, which would be outlined on a flip-chart page. This list of needs then became the agenda from which they gave their entire presentation.

The results of this one
simple change?

The same people, wearing the same clothes, presenting to the same sorts of customers the same products, price points, experiences, and abilities went five-for-six in their next half-dozen new business pitches.

If you want to stop being predictable, talk about the listeners' issues, opportunities, problems, and needs *first*.

If you begin this way, listeners will say to themselves, *"Boy, this presenter is on the mark. They get it. I should listen to that person because he or she is focused on my issues and maybe, just maybe, we can advance the ball today on our problem/ opportunity."*

You will gain instant attention.
Instant differentiation.

So what can you do right now to use this idea?

1. Realize that you can use the important information about your firm as you answer all the listeners' needs and issues. It simply needs to be re-sequenced to be dropped in where it is part of your answer to how you will address each of the listeners' needs. When listeners hear about your organization in the context of what they need, it is truly heard and can make an appropriate impact.

2. Call your listeners and verify just one more time the key needs/issues they want you to address. What are the problems they want you to help them with? Hear one more time how they define their needs.

3. Get them to e-mail you or fax you this list of needs.

4. Also ask them to prioritize their needs and issues, so you can address them in the order they believe is most significant to their situation.

5. Promise the listeners that you will begin your presentation by listing on a flip chart the set of needs they send you and that you will address them in the order they want. (They will hardly believe their ears, because they are so used to the typical scenario described earlier.)

6. Start your presentation by delivering on the promise: Write the list of needs they sent you, in the order they prioritized them, on a flip chart before they come into the room. Leave it on the flip chart so they see it when they walk into the room. They will say to themselves, "This is what was supposed to happen. So far, so good."

7. Open with the normal, "Thanks for the opportunity to speak to you today."

8. Then immediately say, "You asked us to address your issues/needs in this order, and we are prepared to do that. Before we begin, have there been any changes that we should know about, so we can also address those concerns?"

9. If there are any additions or changes, such as order of priority, write them on the flip chart.

10. Then ask if they would like you to present in the revised order. You are showing them that you are not only flexible enough to respond to changing priorities, but you can also adapt if the priorities change yet again. They will be amazed you can. It proves you are there for them; you are there to help them with their needs, not just there to tell them your story. This is Consultative Presenting.

11. Your job right now is to re-sequence all your information in the presentation you have prepared to flow in the order required to explain how your ideas can address their needs. To do this, your visuals must be sequentially flexible. This should not take long. The visuals are in your computer. Just reorder them so you can address the needs of the listeners in the order they requested. Most of the required changes can be executed by using the "cut and paste" function in MS Word, once you have your listeners' needs clearly defined.

12. You will give your same presentation, but in a much more listenable form. This will make your presentation stand out from the others, and it will be much more interesting to your audience.

13. Now go make the call to your listeners. Make the offer to address their needs in the order they wish. Get them to send the list to you. And promise to start by addressing their needs in the order in which they have prioritized them. This tactic is easy to accomplish, and it makes you stand out right off the bat. In fact, this tactic makes you stand out even before the presentation begins.

Define one or two needs you believe they have that they do not have a clue they have.

Typical Situation

We have addressed all the needs you listed and in the order you requested. We believe we can bring solid experience and a great team of people to the situation you explained. And we believe we can help you get to the position you desire.

Define one or two needs you believe they have
that they do not have a clue they have.

*You may recall that nailing the needs you
finally defined took quite a bit of discussion.
So there has been some real progress
regarding identifying the real issues as you
see them. We have also pointed out the severe
problems that will occur, in our opinion, if
you don't act with some urgency to install a
new process in your production line.*

*Therefore we recommend you act
per our recommendation.*

**Most presenters have
usually not even addressed
the needs of the listeners
until they are more than
halfway through their
presentation.**

*Let's assume you did a great job of this, per
Tactic 1. Now why not be truly consultative?
Address some issues you believe they have
that they don't even have a clue they have.*

Tactic:2
Define one or two needs you believe they have that they do not have a clue they have.

In the process, you demonstrate you are trying to help them as much as possible by digging deeper. Digging past the request.

Digging far enough to say:

"By doing more homework, we have found out some other issues, and we believe these need to be addressed. In fact, we believe they rank high on the priority list of actions you should initiate to attain your defined goals."

Boy, will they want to talk to you! You are not just talking about how hard you will work for them, but you are also demonstrating your thinking. This differentiating technique is so unique that it many times becomes what the listeners will talk about most after you leave.

Digging deeper   Digging past the request

Define one or two needs you believe they have
that they do not have a clue they have.

"WAIT 'TILL YOU SEE
ALL OF THE BEAUTIFUL THINGS
IN STORE FOR YOU!"

A Real-Life Story

Frank, a senior salesperson for a major national news magazine, was so excited when he called me. He had just gotten out of a key presentation to a prospect, and at the end they had said, "You are the first presenter who thought past what we asked you for. We look for people who think. That is who we want to partner with, pure and simple."

Frank had suggested that his client, a national advertising agency, should look at two additional needs to help its own client with. The client of this national advertising agency was a state business development office. Frank had checked the trade press and had dug deeper into his own large publishing organization and quickly identified two areas where it was obvious that his publication could assist the agency in helping its client, IF the key players at the agency understood these two additional areas of opportunities. These included some database research and additional publications the client could make use of because of special sections.

Frank presented these suggestions after he had responded to what the agency had asked him to address. Then he reviewed the research that revealed these two additional areas of opportunity and how his publication could assist the agency in targeting those possibilities. The agency in turn presented these ideas to its client and looked as if its own representatives had been doing some real consultative thinking by going past the requested assignment.

Define one or two needs you believe they have that they do not have a clue they have.

The advertising agency convinced its client that these additional issues had to be addressed.

Frank enjoyed a much larger sale than if he had presented only what he had been asked to focus on. Plus, Frank laid the groundwork for a long-term relationship with the agency because he had helped its representatives look smart and consultative. Frank made himself stand out by demonstrating that he cared and by doing more homework than had been requested. Once you start offering ideas you believe the listeners need that they don't realize they need, you will never go back to addressing just what they asked for.

Never.

So what can you do right now to use this idea?

1. Ask your entire team what they believe the listeners need that they have not asked you to address. It is not uncommon that you will hear one or more of your own people say: "Well, what they really need is this. It's obvious! Don't you see what will happen if they did thus and so; they would have an incredible opportunity to leap ahead of their competition. Why can't they see that?"

2. Call an editor of the major trade publication in the listeners' industry and discuss current trends. Attempt to discover where your listeners are coming up short strategically. Bounce your observations off the editor and get a reaction. Explore your fresh thinking with this expert, who writes monthly about your listeners' industry. Ask what they believe the companies in that market must do to bring more progress to the industry in general. Trust me, they will have some hot "to do list" ideas.

You can ask what the editor believes the outlook is for organizations similar to the one you are presenting to, if they do not pay attention to these trends. Just keep asking why, and you'll get new, fresh observations you can use.

Editors are a fountain of current information and industry trends. They also must present fresh ideas and write provocatively to engage readers and keep their publication in business. They are usually quite opinionated, so you should get some crystallized ideas that are maybe even outside the box.

3. These ideas will stimulate your own thinking as to how you and your organization can help the listeners by addressing an area that has, up to now, escaped their attention as well as yours. List these new ideas.

4. Start digging. Investigate additional sources to quickly find information that will help define any areas you can zero in on to demonstrate your thinking:

a. You'll be amazed at how much magical information you can unearth by spending one hour browsing the Internet.

b. Have a discussion on the phone with the head of the trade association in which the listeners' company is a member.

c. Call one of the listeners' salespeople. Salespeople, because of their relationships, are usually closest to the truth about what is actually happening in the marketplace. They almost always will have a comment about how their company is missing the target on some critical opportunity, which, in their opinion, will open the floodgates to more sales.

d. Call a competitive salesperson to unearth your client's strengths that are not being used or weaknesses the competition is homing in on and must be addressed.

e. Call key distribution channels to hear about new products, new markets, and new trends.

f. Call a few academicians who teach and publish on your listeners' type of product, service, etc. They may be ahead of the curve about what must change in the marketplace.

5. Create some visuals about these ideas. Crystallize your thoughts. Remember: The listeners do not even have a clue about these ideas. Don't get ready to pontificate; just be consultative.

6. Make these new ideas/observations separate from the information you are going to present based on the needs they have defined.

7. During the actual presentation, after you have addressed the needs they defined, you can say, "We have done some extra digging and thinking, and we believe we have uncovered other issues you may need to address to get to where you defined you want to go. Would you like us to review them before we summarize?"

8. Never leap into any hot news you've discovered until you address what they defined they needed. If you do, they will say to themselves, "Another presenter who did not listen to what we said we needed."

9. Now go and add to what they asked you to address, and demonstrate you can think, not just respond!

Tactic:3

If possible, change the agenda.

Presenters feel good when they have done the work to get their listeners to define what they need. That by itself is a huge accomplishment. Ask any presenter!

Now let's say, in addition, you have done more homework to uncover some needs you believe the listeners have that they don't have a clue they have. In real life this is more than most presenters do. You have a couple of issues you are excited about discussing in the presentation. In fact, you can hardly wait, because you believe you have a home-run observation that will certainly make a dent in their thinking to date.

If possible, change the agenda.

Tactic:3
If possible, change the agenda

Tactic 3 allows you to play with all you know and all you have done to get ready. It is a lucky strike over and above Tactics 1 and 2. Changing the agenda is definitely not a predictable part of a presentation. When you begin with questions, it demonstrates that you are there to help with what the listeners define as significant. You are demonstrating you are flexible about discussing whatever they decide is critical.

In business today, critical issues change very fast because of pace, technology, and global competition. Overnight fast. It is very hard, however, to get a good discussion going so you can change the agenda if you have not done the homework outlined in Tactic 2. IF you have done the homework necessary to define some needs you believe they have that they don't have a clue they have, do everything in your power to change the original agenda.

Then you can demonstrate your ability to be flexible and change to what has been decided at the moment to be a better agenda. This tactic feels very natural, because you are simply bringing up issues that will prove you have done your homework and are focusing on what is best for the listeners.

you are flexible

And when you begin by demonstrating that you have the flexibility to address whatever is now the listeners' number-one need, they sense a true partner. They recognize you as someone who is solely focused on helping them and their organization succeed.

By starting this way, you demonstrate that you can accommodate any last-minute changes the listeners deem critical.

Being able to change your agenda on the spot is a simple, yet powerful, technique. It interrupts the pattern of the presentation and reveals the unique presenter standing at the front of the room. All it requires is some additional homework, so you can probe intelligently. Listeners love it because you are focusing on their interests and hot issues, not yours. It makes for a presentation that is totally on plan, or "on message," as some folks say.

change your agenda on the spot

focus on hot issues

listeners love it

A Real-Life Story

Terri is an engineer at a nuclear waste clean-up facility. She has a PhD and fifteen years experience. One sharp professional! She is naturally inquisitive and has a fantastic track record for attaining her objectives. When we met three months after my first presentation class to her company, she had a smirk on her face. It was clear she was about to unleash a great story.

She described how ecstatic she had been when she tried the idea of demonstrating her flexibility with an already defined agenda. Terri said that she was adamant about making some process changes, so her department could meet its targets. And in the process, she and her department would look good. Ultimately, they exceeded their goals. Here's what Terri said:

"I was loaded for bear. In our presentation, my team and I planned to carefully address all the issues our management believed were critical. I had also done additional research to address other issues I felt were essential to accomplishing my department's objectives. I wanted to demonstrate just how ready and able I was to discuss and act on what I strongly believed needed to be done. Specifically, I had identified changes in two processes that were causing untold problems of quality. I wanted to demonstrate I cared to the core of my being and was flexible enough to tackle the issues in any order.

flexible

If possible, change the agenda.

"I launched into the opening of my presentation to see if the agenda as set by my management, against the issues they had defined, could be changed. Here is how I started:

"'Thanks for the chance to show you what you wanted us to address and in the order that you asked. Since business moves at such a fast pace, is there anything that has changed since you confirmed the needs you wanted us to address? For example, are your priorities the same?

"'Has any activity in our own organization caused any reprioritization?

"'Has any technology been put into the market we service that might cause any additional issues to be discussed today?

"'Have you realized that there is a more current process than we are employing? I found this out when speaking to an editor of a high-tech publication. In fact, he said we were behind the curve in this area based on what we were trying to accomplish.'"

As Terri reviewed the issues, her knowledge of the needs they did not currently have a clue about made her appear to be almost clairvoyant, and she was able to facilitate the discussion on the spot. Her additional digging on subsequent issues she believed crucial to discuss was the intellectual ammunition that allowed her to change the agenda and arrive at the best way to proceed, so her department could meet its targets.

As Terri facilitated this discussion to refocus the agenda, she oozed the confidence that came from having done her homework. Her energy was electric and quite apparent as she delivered a big-time rip about the quality problems and why they simply must be solved in order to meet the targeted outcomes.

She did facilitate the agenda changes. Then she was able to properly address the new order of what all concurred was a better agenda, because she had sequentially flexible visuals. Terri was on the money. She was leading the discussion. In fact, she was leading! She got her recommendation approved and said that the changes were already executed and that her department is on target to meet its objectives.

arrive at the best way to proceed

If possible, change the agenda.

So what can you do right now to use this idea?

1. Call the people I suggested in Tactic 2 to get information that will allow you to generate some needs you now believe the listeners have that they don't realize they have.

2. Create some probing questions regarding the sensitive issues the listeners have asked you to address. Begin with these to generate some discussion that may change the agenda.

3. Let the cat out of the bag as you start to probe for possible agenda changes. Unveil in the discussion some needs they have that they don't realize they have that could be added to the agenda.

4. Be ready to reprioritize needs after you share these new observations, based on the listeners' goals and objectives.

5. Now the 64-million-dollar skill you must have in order to pull this off: You must be able to be 100% totally and sequentially flexible with your visuals. Some media are more sequentially flexible than others. However, all media can be flexible. You must modularize each section, so you can re-sequence quickly and address the needs as they are redefined.

6. Ask for a couple of minutes to make these changes, so you will be presenting on target to the revised agenda. You can suggest everyone get a fresh cup of coffee while you make these changes they have requested.

Tactic:4

Express a singular point of view — a strong opinion.

Typical Situation

A presenter often starts off, gains some momentum, and about five-to-ten minutes into the presentation, a listener may interrupt, saying, "Helen, just exactly what is your point here? We have been listening for some time now and I really don't have a good grip on what it is you are trying to tell us."

When asked this question, the presenter too often responds, "Well, what I think I am trying to tell you is . . ." The biggest frustration for a listener is to decipher what the presenter is trying to say.

What is your point? Even more importantly, what is your point of view?

In the words of Ron Hoff, another author on presentation skills, "If we can't be remembered, we can't be evaluated!"

Tactic:4
Express a singular point of view—a strong opinion.

You will be remembered if you bring a point of view (POV) into your presentation.

I define a POV as "your opinion." It is the single most important idea you want the listener(s) to remember.

Everything flows from your POV. And since most presenters really don't have a laser-clear POV, you will stand out.

Many presenters are nervous. We all feel nervous at some point. The reason: We have not identified the single most important idea we want our listeners to remember.

In this case, we have every right to be nervous.

Do not make the mistake many presenters do, announcing about fifteen minutes into their presentation, "What I think I am trying to say today is. . . ." That does not honor my time as a listener.

We are all being paid to have an opinion about our particular discipline. Not just information from our experience and education, but an opinion. Your POV is your opinion. Your *strong* opinion.

This will be the most important line in your entire presentation. Now, make sure you have one.

A good POV is truly an "I believe" statement. In fact, you must be able to say, "I believe" as you express it or it is probably not an opinion. It is probably the title of your presentation or an agenda of what you are going to cover. It may be anything but an honest-to-God strong opinion.

<u>A powerful POV has three parameters:</u>

- It is short.
- It is benefit oriented.
- It is provocative.

Express a singular point of view—
a strong opinion.

Why short?

• So you can remember it.
• So the listener can remember it.
• So it is easily visualized.
• So it is easily repeated.

Why benefit oriented?

• So listeners wake up because there is a hint that they are
   about to hear something valuable.
• So you hook listeners right off the bat and keep their
   interest throughout your time together.

Why provocative?

• Anything out of the ordinary evokes interest.
• It generates energy and belief in your own "buy-in."
• If you appear as if you have not bought your own idea,
   why should the listener?
• You will automatically start presenting with more zip,
   passion, and clarity. In fact, the more provocative your
   POV, the more natural energy will automatically come
   forth.
• More energy correlates with better closure.

How's that for making your presentation stand out?

A Real-Life Story

Chuck was a senior civil engineer for a giant contractor that built roads, utility plants, dams, and manufacturing plants all over the world. With twenty-two years of experience, Chuck is one of those people who can hold an audience with mesmerizing war stories. In fact, some of Chuck's third-world adventures make you wonder what drives this man, because his life is very dangerous at times. Chuck called and told me this story about four weeks after our first workshop:

"I finally saw the light about what I had been trying to explain for months to my management. During your training, I created a point of view about my strong opinion. Real strong in fact! Then, during the workshop, my classmates further improved it. I gave my boss this presentation as soon as I could corral him after the workshop. You will hardly believe what he told me.

"He said, 'Why haven't you told me this before? I want to move on that idea pronto!'

"I said, 'That is what I've been trying to tell you the last few months, and you never said you understood my idea. So I kept adding more facts to explain. However, I never expressed a clear opinion — a "what I believe statement."'

"That was the difference!"

Chuck went on to say that he had given three more presentations over the next two weeks. All had very clear POV statements. And he got the go-ahead on all of his ideas after only one presentation.

A Powerful POV

So what can you do right now to use this idea?

1. Distill a strong opinion from what you are saying. Identify the single most important idea you want your listeners to remember if they are asked to restate what you said.

2. Make sure it is easy to repeat.

3. Give your presentation to someone in your company. Just a three-or four-minute outline will usually be more than sufficient. Then ask them to help you clarify the POV. Let him or her help you wordsmith it.

4. Make sure a "defining visual" flows from your strong POV (Tactic 5).

5. Write your POV on a flip-chart sheet or card that you tape to the wall, so it remains in sight after you announced it. Listeners can then refer to it and easily hold you to your opinion.

6. Repeat your POV throughout the presentation, using it as a transition. You will maintain control, and you'll stop rambling. This will also dramatically reduce your non-words and fillers, such as "ah," "you know," and "anyway," and you will re-energize yourself each time you repeat it. This will make you stand out because most presenters wear down as they drone on.

Express a singular point of view—
a strong opinion.

As they say on Broadway, you only open once.

**Most presenters
do not have
a laser-clear POV.**

Now you will.

Case closed.

Tactic:5

Create a defining graphic.

Every listener is trying to "see your idea" as you present. If listeners go along with your POV, your singular opinion, they are wondering, what will it look like if we act on your idea? Your listeners cannot help but try and visualize the next step. Our brains do this naturally. In fact, we can't stop our brain from doing this. In addition, as ideas get looked at throughout an organization and move upstairs through various management levels, they must be re-presented by a variety of people. If the same picture is not re-presented accurately each time, your idea will either die or it will live inaccurately. You simply must have a defining graphic if you want your ideas to have a life of their own as they start to be re-presented inside of the organization you presented it to.

Create a defining graphic.

Tactic:5
Create a defining graphic.

Instead of letting listeners create their own picture, help them by presenting THE picture of what the situation will look like once your idea has been put into practice.

A Real-Life Story

I was training people with PhDs in physics who work for a national research center. They were obviously very bright. Their client was the U.S. Department of Energy. These brilliant PhDs felt extremely frustrated that the equally brilliant business-types at the Department of Energy and Congress, who listened to their presentations, were not getting their point.

Then the PhDs added a defining graphic, and it was magic! It helped instantly clarify their POV. In effect, if their idea were executed, what the picture would be.

My client, Stan, called and said in a state of excitement and relief, *"You won't believe it, Bob. The customer said out loud, 'Oh, that's what you mean! I finally get it, Doctor. Now I see the relationship between the tests you want to run and the rationale that the tests may define, making it possible to shorten the lead time for a commercially viable application.'"*

Now Stan and his team could move forward on what had hung them up for so long. Defining graphics can hit home runs for you, too.

Create a defining graphic.

So what can you do right now to use this idea?

1. Consider what your idea is really doing if accepted. Look at it from 50,000 feet up in the air. What will change? What will the outcomes be? Why will this picture be beneficial to your listener? Compare the current picture with the proposed picture. Compare following your recommendation with doing nothing.

2. Create a simple graphic that isolates the essence of the picture. It must not have too much detail. It typically compares the current situation versus the future or doing something versus doing nothing.

3. The graphic must be so simple that the listener can redraw it after seeing it once.

4. It must be able to be drawn on a napkin. This is why this type of defining visual is called a "napkin pitch" in the presentation business. If your pitch can be re-presented in short order, it will have a fighting chance of living.

5. The defining graphic usually has two colors.

6. Give your presentation to a few others inside your organization. Ask them to draw a graphic image on a white board, based on what they hear you saying, so the group can build on the ideas of each other. If no one draws the same thing at all, your message is unclear. No clarity means no representations and no action. Go back to step 1.

7. Have your co-workers present back to you with the defining graphic they created. Together select the best graphic.

8. During your presentation, draw it "live" on a flip chart as you explain the results of your recommendations. You will look very professorial and this will also show your listeners how to construct the visual when they share it with others.

9. To help burn in this core idea, refer to the graphic several times throughout the presentation and use it as a transition.

10. A defining graphic focuses you on the "so what" of your presentation. People buy outcomes more than process. Show them the outcome of your idea by creating a graphic they can't forget.

Tactic: 6

Use more than one type of visual medium.

Typical Situation

Nice to meet you all today. I am ready to give you a presentation that thoroughly explains how I (we) can help you and your organization.

I have put the ideas into PowerPoint (or flip charts, or overhead transparencies, or cards, etc.), so you can follow them easily. When I am finished, we will have plenty of time for questions.

Use more than one type of visual medium.

The presenter is doing what is normal, using one visual medium to present his or her ideas.

It is common, acceptable, and very predictable.
That's the problem.

Today PowerPoint has become the medium of choice for a large percentage of presenters. It has many outstanding features. That is why it has become so popular.

But the problem is that the presenter is still only using one type of visual.

This guarantees that the presentation is not as good as it can be.

It is too ordinary.
Unmemorable.
Everyone does it.

Tactic:6
Use more than one type of visual medium.

Always use two or more different visual mediums.

It makes your presentation less predictable.

Why will two or three different visual mediums benefit you as the presenter?

Since each visual medium forces its own purposeful movement, you will automatically move around more, increasing your energy and the interest level of the listener. No training necessary for how to move. You just will move naturally.

Most presenters look as if they are "velcroed" to the carpet. They just don't move much. At least not on purpose. They may move back and forth but that is pacing, and it distracts the listeners. It appears as if the presenter is locked in an invisible six-foot cage as he paces back and forth. This happens when there's no variety in the media and no reason to move.

Movement will also help you stand out from those presenters who just sit there and read their "deck" to the listeners who are following along (usually reading ahead).

Use more than one type of visual medium.

A Real-Life Story

Susan was head of research for a large media company publishing a variety of magazines in the computer industry. She was a terrific presenter. She loved to present, and it was a joy to work with her. She had become the company's most effective user of PowerPoint and used all of its wonderful features with the latest LCD projector. Her peers and her boss, however, experienced her as "too distant" when she used PowerPoint.

"We never feel we get the real Susan," they told her. "Your visuals are very good and very clear. But it feels like you are on such a roll, we don't ever want to interrupt you and ask a question. Didn't you notice that when our team presented to that large software manufacturer last week, the room got stiff and quiet?"

Everyone thought Susan seemed much friendlier when she presented from a flip chart and white board. They felt more connected to her when she used those mediums and she seemed so much more approachable. She seemed less bulletproof and more human.

The following week Susan presented the meat-and-potatoes portion of her presentation with PowerPoint and used a flip chart to highlight the key concerns of the clients. Later, on a white board, she charted out the time line she promised to keep to get her part of the project finished. Her team told her later how easy it was to follow her presentation and how they enjoyed the energy and movement she demonstrated.

"It was just more pleasant to participate in your presentation with you, Susan. Thanks for a fun presentation. In fact, we've never gotten more out of a presentation on research. It wasn't so dry and boring. You made it come alive. We really advanced the ball today!"

Visual aids force purposeful movement. They generate a natural kind of interaction that increases energy and interest. Use two or three visual aids, and you'll stand out, since most presenters use only one visual medium. This simple change can make a powerful difference.

energy

movement

interaction

Use more than one type of visual medium.

So what can you do right now to use this idea?

1. Realize that, with its professional look and great graphic capabilities, PowerPoint is the most efficient medium for disseminating a ton of information quickly. The other media, however, "connect" you to the listeners better.

2. Decide which media to include in your presentation. They can range from the mundane to the profound:
- Flip chart
- White board
- Cards that stand on an easel
- An eye-catching brochure
- A mock-up of a deliverable, such as a product or a report
- An actual product or a competitor's product
- An enlarged photograph from the listener's web site of one of their distribution locations
- A photograph of their customers you either can pull from their web site or one you can take of anyone who fits the customer's demographic profile
- A process or product demonstration
- An eye-catching prop
- A "slide show" direct from a digital camera through your LCD projector or direct through a TV monitor

3. Start small. Add one new medium to your next presentation and then experiment with others until you find your favorites.

Now decide what you want to use and, as Nike says, "Just do it." You'll be glad you did.

Tactic: 7

Balance high-tech and high-touch visuals.

I see you have your computer to set up PowerPoint. Did you bring your own projector? Good. Ours is old and doesn't work too well.

I will be back in ten minutes when you are all set up. Okay?

Anything else you need?

Because of all its advantages, PowerPoint is the standard and PowerPoint is predictable. In fact, the presenter may have customized the presentation in the United Airlines club on the way in, so it has all the right names and numbers in it.

And it works.

But it's predictable.

Balance high-tech and high-touch visuals.

BALANCE HIGH TECH AND
HIGH TOUCH VISUALS.

 IDEA:

PASS OUT FORTUNE COOKIES DURING YOUR PRESENTATION. INSIDE OF THE COOKIES WILL BE A MESSAGE GEARED SPECIFICALLY TOWARD YOUR POTENTIAL CLIENT. IT MAY CONTAIN THE CLIENT'S MISSION STATEMENT, COMBINED WITH YOUR COMPANY'S PLAN TO INTEGRATE THAT INTO A PROJECT. OR IT MAY CONTAIN ONE OR MORE CLIENT PROBLEMS WITH A ONE WORD SOLUTION.

Tactic: 7
Balance high-tech and high-touch visuals.

By "high-tech" I mean a presentation using PowerPoint exclusively.

"High-touch" refers to mediums, such as flip charts, white boards, cards, posters, banners, photography mounted on a card, and a technique I call "Immersion Presenting."

The immersion technique is an idea originated by Walt Disney. The definition of Immersion Presenting is that "when the presenter is finished, the listener can see 100% of the visuals." You create visuals on paper and tape the paper up on a wall, covering each visual. You reveal each visual as you present it, so the listener cannot read ahead. This facilitates ease of focused exchange—the goal of all presenters.

The basic idea is to use *both high-tech and high-touch.* Most presenters seem to use one or the other and you seem far more interesting when you use both.

High-tech visuals are the most efficient way to present a massive amount of information.

High-touch visuals connect you to the listeners better. They foster more interaction. They are less formal and more conversational. This simple idea will make you stand out because you will be more engaging and energized. You will efficiently deliver your information while retaining a personal touch. This is one of the quickest ways to change and avoid being predictable.

the immersion technique

1. Tape the two top corner edges to the wall.

2. Grasp the bottom edge and bring it slightly above the top edge, creating a 180-degree curl in the middle of the page. Do not crease the paper.

3. Tape the half-size page closed with one or two small pieces of tape.

4. When you're ready, remove the pieces of tape at the top and unfold. Reveal each sheet in this way as you present.

5. If you like, tape the sheets up so that the titles (in large letters at the top of each page) are visible. This way your audience can see your agenda in advance, and can easily understand exactly how you will move through your topics. (If you do this, hold onto each page as you remove the tape, so that the whole page doesn't get pulled off the wall.)

Balance high-tech and high-touch visuals.

A Real-Life Story

Samantha was a top-rated service specialist in a national office products company and a true road warrior. It was not uncommon for her to help improve reliability on an array of high-tech products, such as copiers, fax machines, and scanners, because of a better maintenance program. This dramatically improved the efficiency of the small-business clients in her territory.

Samantha had an unusually important presentation to renew an annual maintenance agreement with her second-largest client. They had told her they were shopping around for the best value in maintenance, and she would have to make a good case for why they should continue to give her 100% of the maintenance contract. Samantha decided it was the time to look different. It was the time to make her past experience with this client jump off the page during the presentation, so Samantha would be the obvious choice going forward.

She loved PowerPoint and had used it exclusively in the past when she presented the situation and her proposed solutions to her client base. One reason she liked PowerPoint was that she was able to "cut and paste" from previous presentations as she developed a new one for a client who had similar issues. It also helped her convey a tremendous amount of information.

When Samantha took my training, she experimented with other visuals like props, flip charts, wall banners, and paper taped to a wall that she could continue to refer back to. She had used some of these after the training, but this would be the first time she really stretched herself.

Samantha called after winning the entire maintenance agreement. Here's what her clients said:

"You were so real and so easy to follow. We really liked the way you reviewed the key issues by writing them on pieces of paper taped to the wall. Then you kept us glued to the demonstrations by using actual equipment as part of your presentation. Your normal style went up a big notch because you connected in a more personal way than ever before. We were proud we had you doing our work, and we felt we actually got to know you better as you went around the room, using your different visuals to keep the message on track, and not losing any of us in the process."

Samantha added that the crowning comment came when they asked her to come in and repeat the entire presentation to their own service/salespeople as an example of how to be more clear, interesting, and engaging.

"I just did it again, and it was a blast!"

Balance high-tech and high-touch visuals.

So what can you do right now to use this idea?

1. Carve up your presentation into the pieces that belong in PowerPoint and the ones that can be visualized in the high-touch mediums you prefer. For example, the background data necessary to help platform your rationale goes into PowerPoint, while the meeting agenda can reside on a flip chart.

2. Make sure you fully utilize all of the wonderful features of PowerPoint, such as:

- Builds

- Animation

- Video

- Tabular data converted into charts and graphs

- Clip art (Be sure to download some fresh clip art. We have all seen the standard art that comes with PowerPoint. You can also download your own clip art from web sites and books you have purchased. Make sure to credit the source. Cartoons from magazines are a hit with most audiences and give your presentation uniqueness. You may only use these with permission, but the extra effort is worth it.).

- Photos you have taken of the listeners' distribution channels, customers, competitors, products on display in the store, people using the product, a photo of you speaking to important people as you got ready to give this presentation, etc. The list is endless and easy to generate, even on short notice.

3. Prepare most of the high-touch visuals in advance.

4. Identify which ones can be created "live" as you present. You can pen out your point of view, for example, on a flip chart as you open the presentation.

5. To help the listener understand and remember your main points, tape the flip-chart pages on the wall, so you can refer to them often during the presentation.

6. Create a set of Immersion Sheets that have the essence of the entire presentation on them.

7. Tape the Immersion Sheets to the wall before the listeners come into the room.

8. Reveal the Immersion Sheets one at a time as you present, so the listeners cannot read ahead. This medium is called storyboarding by some folks and is a fantastic technique because all the visuals remain in sight at the end of the presentation. This is the best visual for your summary because it allows the listeners to see the essence of your idea, so they are more easily able to ask you focused questions. It is also the best medium to foster exchange and connection.

Kinko's is a handy source to make these Immersion Sheets. Of course, you always can pen them out with fat flip-chart pens, roll them up, and carry them with you. Cheap, fast, and obviously made just for the listener, who always knows what part of the presentation is canned and what part is personal.

Variety is still the spice of life. Mix high-tech with high-touch and **stop being predictable.**

Tactic:8

Be more conversational, less presentational.

Most presentations are organized like this:
90 percent formal presentation
5 percent summary
5 percent questions and answers (Q&A)

If the presenter runs a little long, the Q&A is cut short. Listeners hear the story but little discussion takes place. Often they must call another meeting to discuss what was presented and make a decision on the ideas in question. You will be insanely more effective if you make your presentation more interactive. Insanely.

Be more conversational, less presentational.

Total Time Allowed

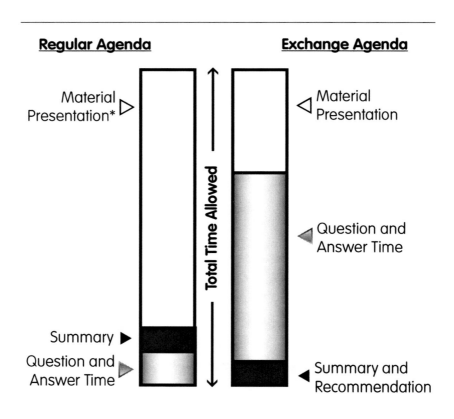

Regular Agenda

Material Presentation* ▷

Summary ▶
Question and Answer Time ▶

Total Time Allowed

Exchange Agenda

◁ Material Presentation

◀ Question and Answer Time

◀ Summary and Recommendation

*This is optimistic. Most presenters go overtime.

Tactic:8
Be more conversational, less presentational.

Consider organizing your presentation in a way that top-level people love. I call this the Exchange Agenda. The more exchange there is, the better the chance you have of closing. With no exchange, you have no idea how your recommendation was received.

When you use an Exchange Agenda, your presentation becomes a serious and involved conversation with your audience. You build rapport quickly and easily. And you stand out from other presenters from the very beginning because you listen to and interact with your audience far more deeply and frequently. The main result is that they develop trust in you because they have a chance to truly talk to you, rather than listening to you drone on.

Be prepared to spend more time preparing when you use the Exchange Agenda. You must anticipate the questions each member of your audience is likely to ask—and obviously you've got to have a good answer ready for each one. You'll also have to answer the most important if unasked question: What's in it for me (WIIFM)? The Exchange Agenda is the very best way for your audience to see for themselves that you really know your stuff.

anticipate the questions

A Real-Life Story

Lawrence was the CFO of a large food manufacturing company. He was famous for his dry and, quite frankly, boring monthly reviews to the top management team. It was always the same from Lawrence. Very predictable. The other members of the executive team would get glassy-eyed, and some would even doze off as he presented. It was embarrassing for everyone. In fact, they called it the "Lawrence dump of the month."

Lawrence also hated these sessions. He experienced considerable nervousness when preparing and delivering these monthly "dumps." Plus he was well aware that his fellow team members did not like how he presented. He felt trapped as to how to improve a painful experience for them and him. He was locked into believing that more data was better. Just keep heaping it on was the only style he knew. It was safe, however, because he could not be accused of not doing his homework.

But the rest of the management team could never remember the information, because it was so painful to sit through his presentations. They went into a brain-dead mindset as soon as Lawrence got up to give his monologue. Since it was heavy with data, it always ran long and left no room for discussion. Plus no one felt like discussing the information. They just wanted to get his presentation over with. As a result, they never made meaningful financial decisions as a team.

After one of my training seminars, Lawrence tried thinking of his presentation as a "planned conversation," rather than as a chance to distinguish himself as bulletproof with tons of data. With great trepidation, he made one change based on what I call the Exchange Agenda. He opened with his key recommendation, limited the formal "data dump" to one-third of the total time allotted, and spent the rest of the time interacting with the team—answering questions, addressing concerns, and discussing relevant issues.

In an e-mail to me afterward, he said the response from his fellow top manage-ment team was nothing short of miraculous.

"What's in it for me"

"They told me it was as if there was a different person up there. They had a chance to interact with me, and the entire twenty minutes was a conversation about the financial status of our firm, not an oral dissertation from a PhD. They said the time flew by and they got a chance to ask me questions. And I was so well-prepared that they even gave me thumbs-up on the new technology I believed was necessary for faster financial reporting back into the divisions, so they could manage their inventories more effectively."

Be more conversational, less presentational.

FOCUS ON BEING PRESENT.

If you think everyone's listening, they're not.

Here's why:

Our brains work at
800 words per minute.
Therefore the audience
is most likely
to drift out of the room
while you are presenting.

They can't help it.

Make sure you continually
"bring them back in"
through forced exchange.
Plus make sure your
content is full of
WIIFM.

Be more conversational, less presentational.

So what can you do right now to use this idea?

1. Dramatically reduce the formal part of your presentation to one-third of the total time allotted. If an hour has been set aside, your actual presentation should be no more than twenty minutes, plus a short three-to-five-minute summary at the very end of the hour. Spend the rest of the time interacting with your audience—answering questions, addressing concerns, and discussing relevant issues.

2. Ask yourself, "What would each member of my audience ask me if they were really tuned in to this subject?" It is this step that requires the extra time to prepare. I call it getting ready to "prime the pump," so you can ask the question for a particular listener to get the conversation going. You must get good at this, so you have the exchange we have been talking about. It is necessary to practice how you will ask someone's question, so it feels natural and the conversation gets rolling. It might sound like this: "Bill, I am sure you were going to ask why we changed research methodologies from how we have operated in the past. Well the reason we changed is. . . . "

3. Involve your audience from the beginning of your presentation. Briefly review their situation and needs, in order of priority. Ask for any additions, deletions, or reordering. Tell them exactly how you plan to spend your time together. If you don't, they won't be ready with questions and comments. For example, if you have ninety minutes, explain that your initial presentation will take no more than half an hour, and that the rest of the time will be reserved for questions and answers as well as discussion, concluding with a short summary.

4. Open your presentation by making your primary point: your main idea or offer, your point of view.

5. Recommend a course of action. Say precisely what you want your audience to do or decide and when to force prompt action. I realize it seems unusual to make this recommendation at the beginning of your presentation, rather than at the end. But this is both memorable and profoundly effective because top-level listeners want to know three things:

• What's your point?
• Why is this a good idea?
• What do you want?

6. Ask your audience to respond to what you've said so far—with agreement, questions, concerns, a contract, or with whatever else they wish to express. If they say, "Okay, let's do it," then STOP! Don't present anything more. You've already completed your task— getting people to agree to your offer or idea. Thank everyone and leave. Promptly.

7. More likely, however, people will want to know why they should do what you suggest. In this case, explain briefly, through a short list of support points, why you're making your recommendation and why your audience should say "yes" to it. Do not yet explain any of your support points in detail.

8. Ask your audience which of these points they would like you to explain in more depth.

9. Go into more detail only on those topics your audience requests. If they haven't asked about something, it means they don't need to be sold on it, so leave that item alone.

10. Once you've addressed all of the requested topics, encourage further questions and conversation on any points you've made. This is a good time to insert questions for the audience that they have not yet asked. As you answer, you will demonstrate all your homework and experience.

11. Give a short summary in which you tie everything back to your main idea, your point of view, and your recommendation.

12. Remind your audience exactly what you want and when. Specifically ask for their agreement—their order, their authorization, their approval, etc. Then be silent and let them respond.

The Exchange Agenda is different because you've been in meaningful conversation. The listeners got to know you better and had a chance to develop trust in you. Because exchange increased dramatically, the chance for closure has increased since more questions have been answered.

meaningful conversation

Tactic:9

Ask for what you want.

Typical Situation

Most of the thirty million presentations given every day are given by non-salespeople.

Salespeople know they must close.

Most other disciplines, however, think that they are presenting to "inform," not to close. They have the mindset that it should be obvious what to do once you know the facts. This is what some people tell me with vigor during training and this often comes home to bite them badly.

Non-closers wind up their presentation without a clear, "Therefore . . ."

Their presentation just falls off the edge and the listener has to prod the presenter into what they believe should be done based on all the information they have just heard.

Tactic:9
Ask for what you want.

Realize the only reason for a presentation is to make something happen. You are there to get action, not just to inform.

It is that simple.

Change your view of why you are presenting.

Gestalt psychologists tell us people want closure. They naturally want the next steps, based on the information you just laid out. You are not overstepping your bounds if you make a recommendation.

make something happen

A Real-Life Story

Phil had been a "tough take in training," as those of us in the training business say. Very nice, very smart, and very confident, he battled most of the concepts I dished out. He had a PhD in statistics and worked as a market researcher for a national IT integration service company. He knew what next steps should roll out as a result of what he had discovered in the research he and his department had completed, and he believed it should be obvious to his audience. He didn't feel he needed to demean himself by being too "salesman-like" and ask for action.

He especially did not care for my comment that his presentations always fell off a cliff at the end. I told him, "Phil, you never conclude. You just give good information and then stop. You simply do not address the question: 'Therefore?' or, 'So, now what?'"

Phil disagreed. He just could not buy into the need to have a call to action. A specific recommendation to go forward just did not fit his style.

Phil called me one night about two months after our class. He said that he had been taken to task and severely reprimanded by his president when, at the conclusion of his presentation that day, he had made no clear recommendation about the next steps that needed/should be taken. The president had actually called the report a research "dissertation." And he'd been adamant that the purpose of the research was to help determine if the company should move into a new line of service, when, where, and at what price point.

"He told me I was of no help at all if I did not have a specific recommendation!" Phil said. "He was not pleased with all the money that had been spent with no specific recommended path forward. He went so far as to say he wondered if our department brought any value to the corporation. I was shaking in my boots as I drove home. So sorry for the call at night, Bob. I finally got it. I must have a call to action—a clear path forward."

ask for what you want

So what can you do right now to use this idea?

1. Create a very specific visual that states *who does what when*. Don't forget the *when*.

2. Keep your recommendation short, clear, and specific.

3. Aim for three or fewer action steps. You do not want the recommendation to have a life of its own by making it feel as if you have launched into another presentation. Remember, most politicians have three-point plans.

4. Consider presenting your recommendation earlier in the presentation than you usually would. This "early release" makes it easier for the listener to hear your rationale and agree or disagree—especially important if you know your recommendation will be a surprise. For example, if the listeners think you will be in a specific price/cost range and your price/cost will be substantively different, tell them early. This way they are listening with ears of that price point or cost. Without stating your recommendation earlier than you usually would, you will probably have to repeat much of the presentation.

5. Be very sequentially flexible with your visuals, so you can go anywhere to answer a question smoothly redefined.

6. Use the "early release" idea of your recommendation to engage the listeners with discussion.

7. The next time you present, create your presentation backwards. Write the action steps you want when you finish *first*. In other words, define what you want. Then develop three or four key summary points that support your recommendation. After that, flesh out these summary points with more detail. Finally, create your point of view. This is a simple way to make sure all your support data is relevant and to the point of defending the logical conclusion leading to your suggested action.

define what you want

ask for what you want

Tactic:10

Demonstrate that you are a team.

Most team presentations simply aren't.

They come across like a series of separate monologues from subject matter experts. The smarts are in the room but they are not demonstrating that they are an honest-to-God team. They are just a bunch of sharp men and women gathered to impress the listeners and convince them of their intelligence and their ability to handle both the problems and opportunities of a given situation.

We must bring all our human resources to bear on the listeners' needs. That means a team of your organization's best people. If the listeners are smart, they have asked for the people who will actually be their team, not just a collection of your brightest and best presenters.

The team must look and sound as if they have discussed the listeners' needs and collectively determined the best ideas their firm has to offer. Many times the team is not full of great presenters, and the quarterback, or team leader tries to cover up for the poor presenters by saying too much. This just amplifies the weakest links.

The team also has the challenge of demonstrating synergistic thinking using all of the team's disciplines.

Demonstrate that you are a team.

Tactic:10
Demonstrate that
you are a team.

Your team is made up of specialists with different abilities and focuses. It is essential that you avoid creating a series of separate spiels, each one seemingly unconnected to the other.

A Real-Life Story

Craig, Doris, and Michael worked for a computer software company and had all taken a workshop on presentation skills from me over the course of two years. They were quite good when they started, and all of them became even better. All three loved to be in front of an audience, telling their story. They loved the energy and the challenge of convincing others of their point of view.

About a year after Michael had taken the class, I got a call from him describing a recent disaster that had occurred during a new business presentation. Michael had been the lead presenter and would have become the project manager on the assignment if the team had won. He said everyone had been pumped because the prospective assignment was a perfect fit with their world-class experience. They had the "goods" to deliver in spades—but they had failed.

Here's how he described what happened:

"*Each of us arrived the night before, and we met and walked through the agenda. We didn't really practice, just talked about what we would be covering and getting our act together regarding transitions. This was such a good fit, we believed all we needed to do was make abundantly clear how our experience matched their situation.*

"*Our first mistake was going too long. We had good energy, plenty of hard evidence about experience—probably way too much in hindsight—and PowerPoint visuals that covered the waterfront with data to prove we were the right choice and that we could make this project come to life. Each member of the team seemed obsessed about sharing way too much of their experience and demonstrating why they were the right person for the assignment. We talked at them, rather than with them.*

"*Alex, our CEO, came in early on the morning of the presentation on the company jet, so he did not have the chance to walk through the agenda the night before. During the presentation he told a couple of his favorite stories that ran long but were on message. Then talk about a screw-up! When our CFO answered a direct question from the client, Alex said it wasn't correct! And his answer, which happened to be much different, was incorrect! This was a disaster with a capital "D." Had he been there the evening before, he would have heard the new facts about this issue, and he would have known that our CFO was correct in what she said.*"

Bottom line:

They lost out on a huge software contract worth millions.

The good news is we got together at their office one month later and went through the attached "to do list" and the reasons that all of the "to do's" are necessary.

And yes, they had a much better track record going forward. Much better!

much better

Demonstrate that you are a team.

So what can you do right now to use this idea?

Before we start down the "to do list," note that it is much longer than the other tactics. Reason: there is so much that traditionally goes wrong in team presentations that you will easily be able to stand out by following this list.

Copy it and make it standard operating procedure.

You will love the results.

Remember that the overarching reason for a team presentation is that the subject, the opportunity, and the situation are very important. It is not a matter of the individual competence of each team member. It is all about functioning as a group, so the listeners see and feel the benefits of your team. Here's how to do it:

1. Hold a team-building strategy session.

    a. As preparation for the session, have each team member write down the one or two key questions they feel each member of your audience is most likely to ask them. Obviously, listeners, such as the president, the CFO, the head of HR, and the director of research, are going to ask different kinds of questions.

    b. Each team member should also suggest one or two important questions that the team should prompt or encourage the listeners to ask, because the answers are so powerful and critical to the team's success.

c. At the strategy session, have each member share their questions, as well as the answer they would give to each one. This process identifies the key issues.

d. Next, as a group, agree on which of these specific questions need to be answered first, and which ones aren't as important.

e. Then agree on precisely what the team's answer will be to each important question. This is absolutely crucial. Nothing is more destructive to a presentation than members of a team offering different answers to the same question. This drives audiences crazy and only proves that the team isn't really working together.

f. Decide which team members will answer which questions. Counterintuitive as it may seem, don't simply have your IT person answer all computer-related questions and your financial person answer all the fiscal ones. Instead, demonstrate team synergy by having some team members answer questions not directly related to their specialties. This can be particularly powerful.

g. Finally, use these questions and answers to develop a single, easy-to-remember, tightly focused team point of view (Tactic 4). This central point should express a single strong team opinion, for example, "We believe it's critical to your success that you outsource your international sales and marketing functions by the end of the year." This powerful main point will automatically link together every important question and answer you've identified.

2. Select a quarterback.

a. The quarterback will make sure that everyone comes across as a team, both in the preparation process and the actual presentation. He will lead the audience through the initial interactive process to finalize the needs and ultimate agenda. This person will normally also open and introduce the presentation, set the tone, and provide a burst of energy and enthusiasm that will get team members going and make the audience alert and curious.

b. The quarterback will ask various team members for their input at appropriate moments during the presentation. Occasionally, the quarterback will also direct the flow of information and questioning, but only when truly necessary.

c. The quarterback will also make sure certain questions are brought up; preferably by audience members, but if necessary by people on the team, because the team has home-run answers for them. Ideally, these answers will clearly make your team stand out from its competitors.

d. The quarterback will close the presentation by:

i. Summarizing

ii. Telling the audience exactly what your team wants

iii. Pressing for a specific answer

iv. Helping the audience set a specific time line for future action

3. Select a timekeeper.

a. It works best if the timekeeper is not the quarterback because the quarterback can get on a roll and talk too long. Plus, the quarterback has plenty to do without adding the important mechanic of keeping track of the time.

b. The timekeeper will prepare a list of running times for every part of the presentation. During the presentation, the timekeeper will monitor team members. When a presenter has only two or three minutes left, the timekeeper will give them a prearranged signal. If the presenter is still talking five minutes later, the timekeeper will interrupt politely and ask them to finish.

4. Prepare individually before coming together as a team to rehearse.

a. Each team member must create their own point of view for their part of the presentation, which flows from the team point of view. Obviously, prior to the team meeting, the quarterback has supplied each team member with the team point of view and a clearly defined set of the listeners' needs according to the listeners' priorities.

b. Each team member's presentation needs to address a specific listener's need(s), so the listeners clearly see that what is being presented is relevant to their needs.

5. Rehearse as a group.

a. It is crucial that the entire team rehearse together. If any team member decides they do not need to come to the rehearsal, explain to them that they will not be in the presentation. As a quarterback, you must have the players on your team practice together if they are to play the game well together. Is there really any need to go into the athletic metaphors on this? Those who show up, succeed. Period!

b. Get the timing down for each section. Discover who tends to go on too long and insist that they make adjustments. Each group member must be strict with himself or herself about timing. No one should eat into another's time slot; it simply isn't fair. If necessary, the timekeeper should interrupt.

c. Keep in mind that during a rehearsal, people take about 75% of the time that they'll take when they actually present.

d. Important: don't just rehearse what each presenter will say. As much as possible, have the presenters actually stand up, move around the room, gesture, point, smile, frown, and use their voices expressively, just as if they were addressing an audience and using their visuals.

e. Schedule a full-fledged dress rehearsal using all the team's actual visuals. Without it, the transitions will be painful to observe in the actual presentation.

f. Spend some time and effort smoothing out the transitions from one presenter to the next. Each such hand-off should seem smooth, polished, and logical; however, each should also be very brief. Your presentation time is short and precious; don't use it up on introductions.

g. In addition, determine exactly what each presenter will do with any visuals left over from the previous presenter. Don't make the room into a mess, and don't let presenters simply push aside visuals they don't need for their own presentation. That will give your audience the impression that your team members are not honoring each other.

6. Review and agree on the details. Make sure everyone understands the following:

a. How everyone will get to the presentation.

b. Where the presentation will be held and directions for getting there.

c. When everyone will meet. This should be no later than an hour before the presentation is scheduled to start.

d. Where everyone will meet when they arrive.

e. Who will be bringing what.

f. Who will carry out which tasks in rearranging the room, setting up and testing any equipment, etc.

g. Exactly what everyone will be wearing. You don't want everyone on your team wearing the same blue suit, striped shirt, and red tie. Believe me, it's happened!

7. Make the most of any senior manager on your team.

a. If a senior member of management is part of your team, make sure this person is well prepared and well organized, even if someone else has to do the preparation and organizing for him or her.

b. They must also be well rehearsed. You do not want their part of the presentation to be a recounting of old war stories.

c. Give the senior manager a specific role. Too many times the senior managers are only invited to lend importance to the event. They must have a reason to be there and they must be able to answer two legitimate questions from the listeners:

i. How will you personally touch the process if we decide to choose your firm?

ii. When will we see you again besides the annual golf outing? Sample answer: "I will meet with your president semi-annually to make sure our team is delivering on its commitments to you."

8. One hour before the presentation:

> **a.** Call anyone on the team who has not arrived and find out their estimated time of arrival (ETA).
>
> **b.** Once everyone has arrived, set up the room and arrange all your visual aids. Make sure that everyone's materials are conveniently laid out, but not in such a way that presenters might trip over one another's stuff.

9. Half an hour before the presentation, conduct a final team meeting.

> **a.** Review which client need(s) each presenter will address.
>
> **b.** Review the transitions between presenters and topics.
>
> **c.** Remind the group that each presenter should begin and end by:
>
>> **i.** Repeating the main idea of the presentation, showing how their portion of the presentation ties into that main idea.
>>
>> **ii.** Demonstrating how their part of the presentation addresses at least one need of the audience.

iii. Have each of the presenters briefly review how they will close their portion of the presentation, and how they will tie it clearly to the audience's needs.

d. Review the media and specific visual aids each presenter will use and how they will use them.

e. Review the key questions that will be raised—preferably by audience members, if necessary by the team.

f. When all the presentation and content issues have been addressed, do a last-minute dress check to make sure you all look collected and polished.

g. Finally, just before the presentation begins, remind yourselves of two crucial things:

i. The synergy you bring to the situation must be based on your audience's needs, not on your organization, your team, or your expertise and experience.

ii. You're there to help your audience, not just sell your services, ideas, or recommendations to them.

10. During the presentation:

a. Remind yourself of Stephen Covey's definition of synergistic thinking as "one plus one equals three or more," and his advice to seek first to understand, then to be understood.

b. As you present, listen to what you are saying. If something isn't entirely clear, repeat or clarify it before continuing.

c. Look for opportunities to generate exchange with your audience. Ask and encourage questions. Coax people to share relevant personal stories. Remember that the goal of any presentation is exchange.

d. Ask yourself, "What am I learning that I didn't know at the beginning of this presentation?" Then use this newfound knowledge to focus or strengthen what you say.

e. Make sure all the important questions get asked and answered. If one doesn't, turn to your fellow presenter and ask it yourself. For example, your question might be, "Kim, can you talk a bit about how the process will work under conditions of intense heat?"

f. Remember, in your heart and mind, focus on being present. Be right where you are and nowhere else. Being present will reap untold benefits, because you will feel the pulse of what is really happening in the room and be able to respond appropriately.

11. After the presentation:

A short team huddle will be extremely important to learn:

a. What went well and should be incorporated into the next presentation?

b. What did not go well and should be jettisoned in the next presentation?

c. What did you learn that would make a difference if you move forward?

d. Who were the key players you just presented to?

e. What were their top needs when all is said and done?

f. How can we address their needs even better?

g. Who on our team should do what immediately regarding:

    i. A letter or call back to key players

    ii. Follow-up one week later

    iii. Getting unanswered questions answered

    iv. Any creative follow-up

Tactic:11

Know your turf.

Presenters show up and take what they are handed as far as the room they will present in is concerned. In fact, folks who present a great deal all have war stories about inadequate rooms and how it murdered their presentation effort. Not understanding the turf you'll be playing on guarantees sub-performance. And that can easily make the difference between showcasing your top people and ideas and looking as if you don't have your act together.

To many presenters it seems like an imposition to call and ask about the room before finalizing what they plan to do and which visual aids they will use. Yet, like an athlete, you could very easily show up with the wrong shoes and slide all over due to poor traction because you had not checked the turf you were going to play on.

The room you are assigned to present in may not be the turf of your choice or preference, but you will have the right "shoes" for that room, such as the appropriate visual mediums. So you won't slide around, lacking the traction to move forward, and you will look as good as you are.

Know your turf.

Patrick represented the second largest manufacturer and distributor of automobile windshields in America and was a senior VP of sales for a Midwest glass conglomerate.

He taught me a valuable lesson with this story:

"I was going out to San Francisco to present to a large auto insurance company. Ten days before I was to fly out, I called the executive assistant to the person I was going out to present to and asked her to fax me the layout of the meeting room. I asked her to include information on some specific facts, such as ceiling height, color of the walls, wall surfaces (sheet rock, wallpaper, walls covered with the photos of all the manufacturing plants in the company), windows, window covering to control light, etc., whether the chairs the listeners would be sitting in had casters and could move around and could also swivel, so the listeners could easily see things on different walls in the conference room, if I could dim the lights on a dimmer switch and whether they were on or 100% off.

"Based on the feedback I received, I requested a different room because what I wanted to do to demonstrate our unique ideas would not have gone well at all in that room. I explained why it would be to their advantage to have a different room. They arranged to have the kind of room that would allow me to show what I wanted to. I made sure they understood why a change to a different room would benefit them."

Patrick said he had developed a standard operating policy that included requesting a fax of the "playing field," as he called it. "You see, professional athletes pay a ton of attention to the turf they play on because it makes a huge difference if it's artificial turf or natural grass. The ball bounces differently.

"My presenting turf must be right, or at the very least I must know the turf, so I can adjust my techniques to maximize my effectiveness. Just like athletes who pay a ton of attention to the turf, so must professional presenters know the turf we are going to present on to maximize our effectiveness."

Now here was a true professional. Patrick understood Vince Lombardi's great line: "Pros do the basics well every day, or they are not pros."

Know your turf or suffer the consequences of not delivering to your maximum effectiveness.

Tactic:11
Know your turf.

As the Bible says, "As you ask, so shall you receive." The Bible does not say, "As you need, so shall you receive." Have a standard procedure to ask about the room you'll be presenting in. Ask specifically. If you travel a great deal, delegate the "advance turf work" to someone.

A Real-Life Story

The team walked into the conference room of a large regional healthcare provider, ready to give a presentation on its new software product, which would make the hospital much more user-friendly and efficient.

To the team's utter amazement, the conference table was twelve feet wide and thirty-two feet long.

To top it off, the head of the hospital sat alone on one of the "short" ends. If possible, stand up right now and step off the dimensions of that table (you'll probably have to go outside or find the empty end of an airport concourse to do this). You will instantly see and feel for yourself how rigid and "United Nations–like" it felt and how terribly difficult it would be to interact. You can't even shake hands across a table like that.

No one had asked the simple question, "How big is your conference table?" They had assumed it was a standard size.

It was a very quiet presentation.

No exchange.

No sale.

Know your turf.

So what can you do right now to use this idea?

1. Unlike tennis players who may have to play on grass in a specific tournament when it is not their favorite surface, you can actually alter your turf by rearranging the room to best support your presentation—if you are prepared. Check out the following to scope out a room:

    a. Electric outlets

        i. Where are they located?

        ii. Do they all work?

        iii. Will you need extension cords for laptop computers, projectors, monitors, and other electronic devices?

    b. Lighting

        i. Where are all the switches, and which lights do they control?

        ii. Are there rheostats or simply on-off switches?

        iii. What is the highest level of light possible?

        iv. What is the lowest, aside from darkness?

c. Room dimensions and layout

> **i.** How many people will the room seat comfortably? If this is fewer than the number of people planning to attend, call your contact and ask to change the location. People who are crammed into too small a space will have a hard time relaxing and giving you their complete attention.
>
> **ii.** If everyone attends the presentation, will there still be room along the walls for your visual aids, and for you to stand in front of them as you present? Again, if not, ask to switch to a larger room.

d. Tables and chairs

> **i.** Can the tables and chairs be rearranged or are they mounted in place?
>
> **ii.** Do the chairs have casters and swivels, so they can easily be turned toward any part of the room? What are the dimensions of the table(s)?
>
> **iii.** Are there more tables and/or chairs than you need? If so, should some be removed?
>
> **iv.** How can you rearrange the tables and chairs to best support your presentation?

e. Center stage

> **i.** What area will serve as center stage for your presentation?

> **ii.** Is it large enough for you to work in? If not, ask to switch the location.

f. Visual aids

> **i.** Where will you set up any projectors?

> **ii.** Where will you hang your banner(s)?

> **iii.** Where will you post all your other visuals?

> **iv.** What A/V media are already in the room? Be sure to test any item you plan to use.

g. Windows

> **i.** Do the windows open?

> **ii.** Do they have shades?

> **iii.** If they do, how dark will the room be with the shades lowered

> **iv.** If the windows do not have shades, will overhead or laptop projectors project too dim an image?

h. Miscellaneous

    i. Are markers available throughout the room?

    ii. Is the temperature comfortable?

    iii. Is there a thermostat in the room? Can the temperature be done from another location within the building, or can it be done right there in the room?

    iv. Is there anything unusual about the room or its location (e.g., there will be loud airplane noise if the windows are opened)?

If the room looks like it won't work well, don't be shy about asking to move to a different location. An uncomfortable or inappropriate room can weaken even the best presentation and undermine your efforts. Remember, too, that it is to your audience's benefit if the room works well. So don't feel as if you are being too meticulous or fussy. Get the turf right.

2. Scoping out the presentation room will help you avert a variety of potential problems. But if you're serious about making sure everything goes smoothly, bring the following to your presentation:

    a. Extension cords

    b. Projectors

    c. A roll of write-on cling sheets. These are large (2'x3') sheets of thin, flexible plastic that can be used as portable white boards. Just unroll one and slap it against a wall;

it will cling with static electricity. You can use either dry erase or permanent marker, and there will be no bleed through. Dry erase marker will rub off if the sheet is folded or rolled back up. These cost about a dollar each, come in packages of thirty-five, and are available at any large office supply dealer.

d. A cardboard frame for your overheads that blocks out the unsightly white light that would otherwise surround them.

3. In some cases, you'll be most effective if you completely change your turf and present where the action is. For example,

a. If you're selling computer software, try to present in the IT center.

b. If you're unveiling architectural drawings for a new dining complex, ask to meet in the old dining hall.

c. If you're selling copying machines, gather everyone in the copy center.

Tactic:12

Recheck the mechanics.

Typical Situation

*"Let's not bother them with those details.
Let's just show them how flexible we are
if things aren't quite right."*

*Most presenters have a
"we will take what they give us" attitude.*

Recheck the mechanics.

The hour before your presentation

Tactic:12
Recheck the mechanics.

Always recheck the mechanics and final details.

Remember that presentations are not only intellectual but also physical. Murphy's Law ("If anything can go wrong, it will.") is not in effect in the world of presenting.

O'Toole's Law ("Murphy was an optimist") is more realistic. Follow a mechanics checklist.

You would not want to take off on a commercial airline if the pilots did not go through their checklist. Even if they have flown that route hundreds of times and have 25,000 hours of flying time, they always go through a checklist because of the huge responsibility to do it right. There's no room for an "oops."

A Real-Life Story

Father Arnold Weber is a Benedictine priest and pastor of our church. He is also my mentor and close friend. Father Arnold is a pro in every respect and an outstanding model of a human being.

He had married two of our children and had joined us afterward to celebrate at the Lafayette Country Club on Lake Minnetonka. When our son Michael proposed to his wife-to-be, Molly, we also invited him to officiate.

After the Mass, we all drove to the Northland Inn for the reception. As we celebrated, it dawned on us that Father Arnold was not there. We called the rectory but were told he had gone to our reception. He never showed up.

Even pros take things for granted.

Father had gone to the Lafayette Country Club. He hadn't noticed that for Michael and Molly's reception we had changed to a different location. He assumed he knew where to go. He did not read the wedding invitation closely. He told me later that when he arrived at the country club, another wedding reception was going on, but he was unaware of it at first.

He started to mingle with the people and finally realized he knew no one. He felt embarrassed and angry that he had missed Michael and Molly's reception.

Even pros make assumptions. I have heard many war stories that were equally disastrous. You probably have some yourself. They may be funny later, but at the time they are anything but funny.

Here are some small time bombs to spark your memory:

- People getting lost on the way to the presentation

- No place to park

- Wrong floor in a huge office building

- Did not leave enough time to go through the office building security

- Did not realize they needed to fill up with gas on the way and took a chance they'd make it and ran out of gas

- No shades for a slide presentation

- No room to put the large illustrations the presenter(s) had brought

- No outlets close to the projectors and no extension cords

- So cramped that the room turned into a sauna

Recheck the mechanics.

So what can you do right now to use this idea?

1. Do a final check of names, numbers, and needs. Things can change fast and suddenly in any business. Your ninety minutes may unexpectedly be cut to forty-five. Two of the key people in your audience may be called away on urgent matters. You may be bumped from the best presentation room in the building to an empty office in the basement. If you don't adapt to changes, even last-minute ones, your presentation may be dead in the water before you even open your mouth.

2. Call, fax, or e-mail your contact and ask for a final list of the names of all attendees and their job titles. Ideally, this should be faxed or e-mailed to you for a final check on the spelling of everyone. Also confirm the building address, floor, room number, and directions to the building.

3. Request or confirm any audiovisual equipment.

4. If possible, arrange to visit the presentation room, so you can decide on the best arrangement for seats and visuals. Even when you have received a faxed drawing of the room, an on-site "look see" is worth the time.

5. If the room is out of town, try and have one of your local people go see it and send you digital pictures of the room and a final suggested use of the space.

6. Ask your contact if any significant change has occurred since you were last in touch that might have an impact on your audience or your presentation. These might include a change in competition, personnel, a budget cut or increase, a recent or a pending merger, or a tighter time line.

7. Clarify for the final time the needs of your audience and their organization.

a. For example, you might say: "So that we can be as current and to the point as possible, could you review what you feel your company's or unit's or department's biggest needs are as of this moment?" AND, "Have any of your priorities changed since we talked about your needs earlier?"

b. At the end of your call, say something like this: "I'll be arriving at the presentation room an hour ahead of time, so everything will be ready and we can start on time. Please have all the A/V equipment set up in the room when I arrive." Then ask, "Who can I call if I have any questions about the room?"

8. Prepare table tent name cards for all participants.

a. Make the font at least 72 pt. Most nametags are too small to read at a distance, forcing you to squint, lean forward, and say, "I'm sorry, I can't read your tag; what was your name again?"

b. Decide who sits where. This control is an even more important reason to create your own name cards for attendees.

Tactic:13

Say less, not more.

Typical Situation

Most presenters take their time in the "presentation limelight," attempting to tell all they have learned and experienced since sixth grade. In the presentation business, this style is called "going too deep."

It is also called "Let me be clear about how much work I have done to get ready and all I therefore know about this subject" style. A one-word description of this style is "overbearing."

This is without question a predictable problem with most presenters and therefore a very easy place to differentiate and please your listeners in the process. It makes you even easier to be with and therefore more likable.

Tactic:13
Say less, not more.

The problem of long presentations is easy to relate to when you do a reality check on how fast you lose interest in the many presentations you hear.

You also will be quick to realize how fast you want to ask the presenter, "So now what do we do with this idea of yours?" You've got the idea and want to move forward with some action, yet the presenter is convinced you need more data to support their idea so they keep talking. Painful.

A Real-Life Story

"Are you done, Hank?

"Really?

"What a pleasant surprise that someone actually finished in less time than they had been allowed on the agenda. It's refreshing.

"In fact, Hank, I heard that Albert Einstein once said, 'If you can't say it simply, you don't know your subject.' I believe in that basic tenet, and I am delighted you demonstrated it today.

"I understand your idea. We had time to discuss the ramifications of it and discovered an additional location where your idea would fit.

"Hank, do you realize I have built a career on being brief? Well, if you look back on the presentations I give to our senior staff, the annual meeting, and the quarterly 'all hands' sessions, I try very hard to boil down my message. You did that today. Maybe you have seen that I prefer that style and felt I would appreciate a crisp presentation. Very astute on your part. Remember, Hank, always cut to the chase. I don't have much time, so I appreciate a presenter who doesn't go on forever. That is what I get here in the corner office all too often. It's unbelievably frustrating and a waste of time.

"Remember: Short is beautiful. Short is memorable. Short is tolerable. Short is more pleasant. Short proves you really have done the homework to boil the idea down to its essence, so we have time to discuss and act on it.

"Thanks, Hank!"

Hank relayed that conversation to me after he floated out of his president's office one morning. Hank had done his best to distill many ideas and support points with a very clear and specific next-step recommendation. His president was bowled over.

Hank got his idea approved, even for an additional location. But equally or more important, he did it in a crisp style the boss loved, and he got personal feedback as to the effectiveness of the presentation.

Is Hank's president unique?

Or do most presidents like long-winded presentations? Of course they don't. They love to cut to the chase. And when the presenter doesn't, they feel frustrated with a capital "F."

Say less, not more.

So what can you do right now to use this idea?

1. Realize you have in all likelihood prepared more to say than you need to. So start by cutting 20-30% of the information about your department, your organization, your product, your process, etc.

2. People are more interested in "outcomes" than in "process." Zero in more on outcomes and reduce the information about how you are going to arrive at the outcome—your process.

3. Reduce the number of times you say, "I, we, or our," because you almost always follow those words with a *fact* or a *feature*. For example, "*Our* company has thirteen distribution warehouses. I can assure you that we have the state-of-the-art testing procedures in our manufacturing plants."

4. People buy benefits, not facts and features all by themselves. Increase the times you say, "you and your," because you almost always follow those words with a benefit. For example, "*Your* rejection rate will decrease because of our better quality process and that will reduce *your* warranty claims."

5. If it works for you, try and be extremely brief. For example, speak three minutes when they think it will be twenty. Remember, I said extremely brief. End your presentation with these words: "The brevity of my comments has nothing to do with their intensity."

6. "Tour the edges" of your presentation and take things out, so the listener has a fighting chance to "get it." My friend David Hiser is a famous landscape photographer who lives in Aspen, Colorado. He has had more than sixty-five National Geographic assignments and teaches how to take better landscape photos. In one of his classes he looked through my lens at what I was intending to shoot. He looked back at me and said, "Bob, great photographers take things out of their pictures, so the viewers' eyes go exactly to the spot in the photo the photographer wants them to see. The way they do that is to 'tour the edges of the frame and take things out.'" I have shared this metaphor in training for a long time because I believe that great presenters must do exactly the same thing.

7. Less is always more. Always. Always. Always. And it is such an easy way to stand out from the others! And in the process, make your listeners happier.

Say less, not more.

SAY LESS, NOT MORE.
THEREFORE, REMOVE PERIPHERAL
CLUTTER FROM YOUR VISUALS.

Tactic:14

Look and sound as if you have bought your own idea.

Typical Situation

Many professional presenters are less than passionate.

Some, in fact, look "plastic."

They are thorough. But too often they seem detached from the idea or the real live folks in front of them. They may not even look at their audience much. Their presentation is an organized "data dump" without much heart. Sometimes it is hard to determine if they actually believe in what they are saying. Since this is so common, you will differentiate if you seem sold on your recommendation. If you're not, why should the listeners be?

Tactic:14
Look and sound as if you have bought your own idea.

The key is energy. Not just being energized and walking on the ceiling like some folks you may know. You need to exude focused passion. For decades, communications research has told us that, when it comes to establishing trust and believability, how you sound and look is more important than what you say.

Your passion must be genuine. How you approach this tactic and what you do about it not only will improve your chance to win, but also the general level of trust people will have in you. They want to hear your ideas because you seem to get excited about them and are focused on helping. My definition of selling is "selling is helping." If you focus on helping people, they will take your goods and services. If you don't help them, they won't.

Look and sound as if
you have bought your own idea.

A Real-Life Story

Cynthia was head of public relations in a large Midwestern advertising agency. She had many years of experience and ran a well-respected department.

When she got up to give her opening two-minute presentation in a workshop, she was supposed to include some introductory remarks about what her job entailed, her experience, her education, what she loved to do outside of work, and how she viewed her presentation skills in terms of strengths and areas for improvement.

I was sitting in the back of the room and Cynthia glared at me as she began. Quietly and with emphasis, she said, "I hate to present. I hate it. My co-workers tell me I need to get better at it. But I hate it."

She sat down.

She did not go through any other information. The room became as quiet as a morgue.

Throughout the two-day session, Cynthia tried hard to get the concepts and she was open to the critiques of her fellow classmates, who told her, "You look grim when you present, Cynthia. It is so heavy. It is easy to see you are struggling and not enjoying the process of presenting a PR idea to a client." When she watched her video, Cynthia also used the same word, *grim*.

After my workshops, participants use the ideas and techniques in actual presentations and send me a critique of their efforts. Then I send back a critique of their critiques. It is in this part of the training process that habits begin to change and improvement takes hold.

Well, Cynthia started sending critiques by the bucket load. She was doing everything she could to improve. And she was getting incredible feedback that helped her see that she was, in fact, getting better. Not just a little better, but a great deal better!

When I returned three months after the initial workshop, Cynthia stood up and said, *"You all told me that I looked grim three months ago when I presented. I agreed. I studied my video, and I made a huge decision: I must change or I am in the wrong business. Period. So I decided to do one thing. I decided to make it abundantly clear in every presentation I gave that I cared about my solution and recommendation. I was on fire about how it would help my clients. I cared to the core. It was that simple. They would know I cared about them and their business!"*

She sat down, and everyone just stared at her.

She had made a monumental change. She was passionate when she told us what she had decided to do, and the stories she later shared of her presentations over the last three months were nothing short of sensational.

Look and sound as if
you have bought your own idea.

So what can you do right now to use this idea?

1. Get into the shoes of the listeners and look at the idea you are going to present from their perspective. When you do, you will come across naturally as excited for them and appear as if you have bought your own idea.

2. Revisit your point of view (Tactic 4) and make it as provocative as you possibly can. What do you really believe in your heart of hearts? Words are powerful. My entire methodology in helping you become a better presenter can be summed up this way:

"If you say the right things, you'll say things right."

So you need to review the most important message you want them to remember. How provocative is your point of view? Are you being down deep as direct as you can be? Write a point of view that is a whole lot more provocative than the one you have currently. It will amaze you if you just try. When you say it now you will notice that your energy increases naturally. Your body language becomes more animated. Your passion goes up a notch.

3. Speak from the heart. Have you ever heard someone say, "Would you please get to the heart of the matter?" The heart of the matter is a matter of the heart. If you focus on your feelings and speak more from your heart, you will naturally look and sound as if you have bought your own idea.

4. Be sure to use at least two different visual mediums (Tactic 6). Visual aids force purposeful movement, and movement translates into energy that makes you look and sound as if you have bought your own idea.

5. Tell your story in terms of the consequences if the listeners do not adopt your idea. Fear is a legitimate motivator. Use it, and you will get excited as you describe the consequences and the benefit to the audience if they go along with your recommendation.

6. Get into exchange as soon as possible because we all have a more energized voice when we are conversing than when we are presenting.

Get conversational!

Therefore.....

Now that you've read about the 14 Tactics that will make your presentations insanely effective, the next step is yours. These aren't some half-baked ideas — all of them are conference room tested and *work*.

Here is a parable that may help you overcome your doubts about trying something new in your next presentation and getting better:

When I was a young man, my father came to me and asked me how many push-ups I could do.

"About 30," I replied.

"Could you do 50 someday?" he asked.

"Well, I guess so, if I built up to it and really put my mind to it. Probably right now I couldn't do 50, just 30," I replied.

"But you could do 50 push-ups if you really wanted to." It was as much a statement as a question.

"Yes," I replied.

"Never forget that," he said as he walked away. What a lesson from my dad.

If you decide you want to stop being predictable in your presentations, to stand out from the others, to be insanely effective, then you can. And you will.

Maybe 14 tactics are too much all at once, but pick one and set your mind to improving your presentations. Once you see how easy it is to implement one of these tactics and how effective it is, you'll look forward to further improvement by trying more of them.

We are all responsible for doing our own push-ups. We choose to get stronger and better. In this case, insanely better at presenting!

I believe the best is yet to come if we just try.

Bob Boylan
Carbondale, Colorado
June 2011

About the author

Bob Boylan is a nationally recognized presenter who has been putting his professional objective, "to deliver training that takes," into practice for 30 years. Through his company, Successful Presentations, he has been teaching corporate senior executives across the United States how to give insanely effective presentations.

His passion is to be an inspiring coach and to enjoy the ride. In fact, this is the focus of his entire life. He strives to advance the well-being of anyone he comes into contact with by being that inspiring coach for them.

Bob's mission statement — Live a God-directed, passionate, purposeful life focused on the present — will shed some light on why Bob has written this book. He knows it can help you to be as good as you think you are and to enjoy the ride as you help others see how your idea benefits them.

He lives in Colorado with his wife, Linda, and their dog, Thunder.

Contact Bob:
Bob Boylan
424 Settlement Lane
Carbondale, Colorado 81623
(970)309-5592
bobboylan@me.com
www.bobboylan.com